THE PRISONER IN THE THIRD CELL

BOOKS BY GENE EDWARDS

First-Century Diaries

The Silas Diary
The Titus Diary
The Timothy Diary
The Priscilla Diary
The Gaius Diary

An Introduction to the Deeper Christian Life

Living by the Highest Life
The Secret to the Christian Life
The Inward Journey

The Chronicles of Heaven

The Beginning
The Birth
The Escape
The Triumph
The Return

Healing for the Inner Man

Exquisite Agony
A Tale of Three Kings
The Prisoner in the Third Cell
Letters to a Devastated Christian
Dear Lillian

In a Class by Itself

The Divine Romance

Radical Books

Revolution: The Story of the Early Church
How to Meet in Homes
The Christian Woman . . . Set Free
Beyond Radical
Climb the Highest Mountain

Other Books

Christ Before Creation
One Hundred Days in the Secret Place
The Day I Was Crucified as Told by Jesus the Christ
Your Lord is a Blue Collar Worker

THE PRISONER IN THE THIRD CELL

by

Gene Edwards

TYNDALE HOUSE PUBLISHERS, INC.
CAROL STREAM, ILLINOIS

Visit Tyndale's exciting Web site at www.tyndale.com.

TYNDALE and Tyndale's quill logo are registered trademarks of Tyndale House Publishers, Inc.

The Prisoner in the Third Cell

This book was formerly published by The SeedSowers (Christian Books Publishing House), Auburn, Maine 04210.

Scripture quotations are taken from the *Holy Bible*, New Living Translation, copyright © 1996, 2004, 2007 by Tyndale House Foundation. Used by permission of Tyndale House Publishers, Inc., Carol Stream, Illinois 60188. All rights reserved.

ISBN 978-0-8423-5023-5

Printed in the United States of America

16
20   19   18

*To My Youngest
And Much Loved Daughter,
Cindy*

It has been said that it is impossible to forgive a man who deliberately hurts you for the sole purpose of destroying you or lowering you. If this be true, you have but one hope: to see this unfair hurt as coming by permission from God for the purpose of lifting your stature above that place where formerly you stood.

Prologue

"THE NEW PRISONER HAS ARRIVED, CAPTAIN."

"Is the rumor true?" the captain responded.

Without answering, the guard held up a piece of papyrus for Protheus to see.

"Herod has lost his mind. He will yet be found as mad as his father.

"Making *this* man a prisoner," he continued, "may very well set off a revolution. The common people are enraged."

"Sir, forgive me, but I must speak. I do not like this," said one of the guards in a voice shaking with emotion. "I do not want him here. I do not want his blood on my hands. I fear that man. I listened to him once, in the desert. I fear what God might do to us for imprisoning such a man."

"Do your duty, soldier. Prepare a cell."

"Only one is empty, sir."

"Prepare it then."

"There is nothing to prepare, sir. It is the *third* cell."

"The pit? We shall see a holy man of God vanquished to *that*?"

"Sir, there is something about all this I dislike more than anything else."

"What is that, soldier?"

"I dread what we are going to have to listen to from the other two prisoners when they find out who is in cell three."

"I cannot say I disagree with you," sighed Protheus.

At that moment the door at the head of the stairs swung open. In the doorway could be seen the silhouette of two soldiers and a prisoner.

"I wonder how long Herod will let him live," thought the captain to himself.

He who takes up the sword perishes by the sword. He who refuses to take up the sword perishes on the cross.

Chapter 1

ELIZABETH OPENED THE DOOR to her home, there to be greeted by a young kinsman from Bethlehem.

"I have an urgent message for you from Joseph and Mary."

"Come in," responded Elizabeth. At that moment Zachariah entered the room carrying a young three-year-old boy in his arms.

"I have a message and a small package, both from Joseph and Mary."

"Please," said Elizabeth. "My eyes have long since lost their ability to read such small letters."

The young man broke the wax seal of the small scroll, cleared his throat, and began.

"Strange things have taken place in our lives of late, events as unusual as those that brought forth the birth of your son and ours. We had a visit from three Babylonian astrologers just yesterday.

Then, last night, Joseph had a dream, a very disturbing dream. In it, our son was seen in grave danger from the wrath of that monster, Herod the Great. We are departing Bethlehem at this very hour. Joseph and I are going to Egypt, there to remain until this dreadful danger, whatever it is, passes.

"But our son is not the only one in danger. We fear that John is, also. Perhaps all the young firstborn children in Judea are in danger. Elizabeth, we urge you and Zachariah to leave Judea immediately. Go where you wish, but your nearest, safest hiding place is the desert. With this letter we are sending a small package. If I do not explain, you will wonder forever what a poor carpenter and his wife are doing owning gold. The Babylonian astrologers gave several gifts to us. One of them was a casket of gold coins. We are sharing them with the three of you. Please, in the name of our God, flee Judea today. Tomorrow may be too late. We will try to find you on some better day when, hopefully, we return from Egypt."

The letter was signed by Joseph and Mary.

With that, the young man handed a small leather pouch to Zachariah, which he quickly opened. Inside the pouch were several gold coins. For a moment no one spoke.

Elizabeth, ignoring the gift, broke the silence. "I am not

surprised about Herod. The enemy of God would do just such a thing. We must leave immediately."

Zachariah now addressed the young courier.

"Go. And tell no one of this." With those simple words, the youth bowed his head in respect and departed.

"You are right, Elizabeth. We must leave for the desert immediately."

"How can we survive out there? In order to be completely safe, we must go far into the desert. Can anyone *survive* out there?"

"Elizabeth, it will be a difficult thing for all of us, to say the least. But the Essenes survive out there. They have families; they have children; they have homes out there. Our son *will* survive." Zachariah then chuckled, "Perhaps you and I may even survive there, at least for a little while."

Chapter 2

THE WINDS WERE DEADLY. The heat was more than Zachariah or Elizabeth ever imagined. Canyon walls were like a furnace. Even the blowing sand scalded the face, trying, it seemed, to destroy anything that dared walk into that living furnace. Water was scarce, food nonexistent. In the midst of murderous heat, Zachariah had fainted on several occasions.

Finally, after a week's journey into that boiling hell, the three wayfarers arrived at one of the Essene villages. After several days of rest, they penetrated even deeper into this oven of sand and rock. At last they came to the largest of the Essene settlements.

The three were received with gracious reserve by the sober-faced Essenes. Within a few weeks the elderly couple and their young son had become a part of this strange community of religious stoics.

Zachariah became ill almost immediately. Nowhere in this inferno could he find a hiding place from the all-pervasive temperatures. The old man knew his death was but a matter of days. His last hours were spent being cared for by women of the village who mercifully wrapped his body in wet rags. Finally, late into the night when heat was at its lowest, Zachariah gave his life up to God, leaving a widow and a small child.

During the ensuing years, young John took his place among the Essenes, eventually becoming one of them. From the beginning, the lad seemed to have a natural disposition for the communal life of this desert hermitage.

The wilderness heat eventually took its toll on Elizabeth, for the elderly did not live long in this scorched world. Even as Elizabeth's strength was waning and her steps grew fewer, word came that Herod was dead. Immediately she made plans to return to her home in the cool hills of Judea. With her last good strength, and the aid of several Essenes, she and her son returned safely to her Judean home. But not long after John's twelfth birthday, Elizabeth joined Zachariah in death. John was now an orphan. Elizabeth's closet kinsmen buried her not far from that very place where an angel once visited her and told her that she would bear one of the most incredible children ever to make entrance into this world.

Where would John live now that his parents were both dead? Who would raise this boy to manhood? These were the questions that filled everyone's mind as John and his kinsmen returned to his house.

Chapter 3

"JOHN, WE GRIEVE for the passing of your mother." The voice was that of Hannel, one of Israel's most devout laymen. "Nonetheless, a decision is in order. Tomorrow each of us must return to our separate homes. It is for you to decide which one of us you will live with. Though I am not one of your close kin, I have come here because I know of your devotion to the Hebrew religion, and I have spoken often with your mother about adopting you if the providence of God ever brought forth such a need.

"John, I am very aware of how you feel about your future, that you must one day serve God. In my judgment, the best possible course for you is to come live with me. God has been very good to me, John. Ours is a very devout home. There is prayer; there is fasting. My entire family is devoted to God. I even own several scrolls of holy writ. Few homes are so honored.

"I pledge to you now, in the sight of your relatives, that you will be trained by the best of the rabbis. I commit to you the promise of the best religious education possible. We have a large home. It is quite comfortable. You may spend as much time in prayer as you wish. You may come and go in pursuit of your religious training as you please. When you reach the age of twenty-one, if you desire, you may go to the temple in Jerusalem and study under the Pharisees or be trained to become a temple priest. Though you are of the tribe of Judah and not a Levi, you would be allowed into any of the religious orders, including the Levitical priesthood, because you have taken the vow of the Nazarite."

Hannel paused. John said nothing, nor did he betray any of his feelings.

It was Parnach, a cousin of Zachariah and a man of influence, power, and wealth, who spoke next.

"John, it is true that you may wish to continue to pursue your Nazarite vow. On the other hand, the day may come when you might decide to take some other direction in your life. If you would come to live with me, I will promise you the best education in Israel. I need not tell you of my place in government. I am in the highest echelon of power. You will grow up among the most influential men in our country, for my friends include even its greatest rulers. I have position, prestige, and access to power. Whatever your goal in life, as a member of my house you will be friends of those men who have the greatest influence to help you bring about your goals. I would strongly urge you to come and be part of my household."

Once more John said nothing.

Now it was Joseph and Mary's turn. Mary spoke.

"John, we have very little to offer you. Mostly, the companionship of your cousins. We have a large family. You and my oldest son have always enjoyed one another's company. But if you would come with us, you would work in a carpenter's shop. I suppose in the light of what these men have offered you, it would be wise for you to go with one of them. I am almost embarrassed to invite you to our home. As I said, we are poor, but you will be loved."

"I know," responded John finally. "If I must choose between Hannel, Parnach, and your family, then I would choose the latter."

"Then you will come and live with us?"

"No," replied John, looking calmly into the face of Mary.

Mary inadvertently slipped her hand to her mouth. "It's the Essenes, is it not?" Mary paused, and her face signaled that she desired a clear response.

"Yes, it is. I belong there."

A moment of silence ensued.

"John," continued Mary, "perhaps you do not know this, but several Essene families have moved to Nazareth. Do you remember the two little boys you used to play with there . . . and oh, yes . . . and that little green-eyed . . ."

"Mary," interrupted John, speaking strongly, almost sternly, and very much out of character for a Hebrew lad. "I know what I am to do. The Lord has made this very clear to me. I am to return to the desert, and I am to live there." John now turned toward Hannel and Parnach.

"I wish to thank both of you for your kind offers. You have all been gracious and caring. Thank you for your concern for my future. Nonetheless, I know where I belong. I am returning to the desert."

Once more John turned to face Mary.

"You are my mother's closest friend. She loved you dearly. She spoke often of you. Nonetheless, I must leave here immediately, *alone*. The Lord has taken my father and my mother. I have absolutely no obligations. I have no brothers or sisters, no grandparents." John paused. "You must not worry about me; and though it may seem to all of you that I have simply disappeared, I will be well. God *will* take care of me.

"I am not sure of much, except that I *must* live in the wilderness until God tells me otherwise. This I also know: Out among the Essenes I will discover what it is that my God wishes me to do. The desert will provide me with the answers. My preparation for His will is not in a city nor a village, but a desert."

The next morning a boy not yet thirteen bade good-bye to Parnach and Hannel, to Joseph and Mary, and to his second cousin who was a year younger than he, who bore the name Jesus.

Chapter 4

JOHN TOOK HIS PLACE once again among the Essenes, but allowed no one to adopt him. He lived alone. To provide his meager needs for food, water, and clothing, he worked with his hands.

Never once in the coming years did John touch wine. His hair grew, uncut, from the day of his birth. But because it was the one possible source of pride in his life, he gave even his long raven hair the minimum of attention, obscuring its length and beauty.

Much of this time John spent in prayer and fasting—so often so that his fingers sometimes turned purple, and he was sometimes so weak that his legs could no longer support his frame. Frequently he spent whole days and nights in unbroken prayer, doing little to protect his body from the harsh elements of the wilderness. Austere was the way he lived; stern became his demeanor.

As the years passed on, John began spending his time

wandering the desert. There the fierce sun leathered his face and turned it to craggy wrinkles. By the time he reached manhood, the son of Zachariah and Elizabeth looked far, far older than his age. To John, such things were a small price to pay, for his long treks into the desert were his most coveted times. There he could spend uninterrupted hours alone with God. The howling wind, the furnace heat, the baking sun, and the cutting sand became his closest companions.

As he approached the age of thirty, when, by tradition, holy men might end their training and enter the ministry, John was one who could hear the voice of God within the desert wind, see His face within the sun, and feel His presence in the blowing sand. He was by now both a mystery and a legend among the Essenes. Few men, the Essenes were certain, had ever lived their lives so completely before God. Few men had abandoned every human comfort to be so utterly unhindered in their pursuit of knowing the Lord. In the minds of the Essenes, and even among some of the nomadic tribes, there was no doubt that a prophet was being raised up in their midst. The desert was giving birth to a man of God.

Such a man as John the world had rarely seen. His devotion to God was absolute; his life was void of all except his call to speak for God. He knew no family life, lived without entertainment, without friends, without companionship. The thought of a wife, a home, or children never crossed his mind. Everything within John was for God. The devotion of an Abraham, of a Moses, of an Elijah, of an Elisha, of an Amos, paled in the presence of this single-minded celibate whose only friend and companion was his Lord.

Never before had the world seen anything like John, nor was it likely to see such a man ever again.

One evening, while standing upon the sandstone cliffs that overlooked the Dead Sea and watching a blazing red sun set behind jagged hills, a voice from heaven spoke to him.

> *"John, the fullness of time has come. What you have lived your entire life for is at hand. Go. Proclaim the Day of the Lord. Pull down the mountains; fill in the valleys; prepare a highway for the Messiah. Go, John, now. Look neither to the right nor to the left. Let there be nothing else in your life. No one has ever carried so great a responsibility as do you at this hour.*
>
> *"Proclaim the coming of the Lord!"*

Chapter 5

THE NOMADIC CARAVANS WERE the first to come face-to-face with the desert prophet. Their eyes registered unbelief as they gazed upon the sight of such an emaciated creature. Their first thought was simple enough. "He is some madman who wandered into the desert." Or, more charitably, "The heat has driven one of the Essenes quite mad."

Obviously this nameless man was a Jew; but he wore the garment of an unclean animal, the loathsome camel. And it was soon rumored that for food he ate locusts—a food used by only the poorest, most impoverished people.

His outward appearance declared him a lunatic; his words declared him a prophet. His hair, unkempt, reached almost to his knees. His face was that of an old man, but his voice thundered with the vigor of youth. His eyes flashed the burning fire of the desert.

Despite themselves, men could not but stop and stare . . . *and* listen. The voice rang clear. The words were majestic and bold, almost poetic. There was power in every word. The man himself projected a dignity and integrity almost beyond the grasp of human understanding.

The caravans slowed and formed into a circle around the man. Every soul strained to hear what this man had to say.

And what these desert travelers heard resonated with their own deepest feelings. At the same moment, his words convicted each of them. Everything the man spoke was unnerving. What he predicted was impossible, but what he demanded was even more incredulous. John was not only demanding radical change from his hearers, but he was demanding it right there, right then.

No one, they were sure, would take this man seriously.

The caravans would move on, but others would come; and they, too, would stop and listen. And each caravan, when at last it exited the desert, carried with it the reports of a madman or prophet out in the desert, preaching to all who dared paused to hear.

"Why does he not come into the villages to proclaim his message? Does he not know all respectable prophets preach in the marketplaces where people can hear them? Does the fool think people are going to go out there in that infernal hell to hear him? What person in his right mind is going to that pathless wilderness and standing beneath the blistering sun to listen to a man make demands no one is going to respond to. He is mad, all right."

Yet it happened. Some in the caravans, on their return voyage, would search out the desert prophet. Common folk in villages on the edge of the desert made their way out to hear him. Seeking hearts, empty souls, hungry spirits—desperately longing for something they knew they did not have—dared to take their empty lives into that uncharted wasteland to find *The Prophet.*

At first only a few heard him, but they came back to tell their friends of what they had experienced. Rumors about this wildman spread throughout all of Judea and Galilee.

Listeners came first in ones and twos, then by scores and hundreds, and then by thousands. They came on foot, across burning sands. Their numbers grew daily. Some enterprising men were soon scheduling whole caravans into the desert to hear this man.

They all listened. Some wept. Others fell earnestly to their knees. Many cried out in loud voices for undeserved forgiveness.

Others cheered. No one jeered. Not a critical word came from any mouth, at least not among the common people.

Yet those who never heard him, who lived in the far-off city of Jerusalem . . . *they* judged him, tried him, and convicted him . . . without having seen nor heard him. The verdict was simple. And familiar. It is laid on every nonconformist of every age. "He has a demon."

A few came and sat down right at his feet. Their purpose was clear: These men wished to be John's disciples. And so it came to be.

This handful of disciples would take on John's lifestyle and become his constant companions. Like him, they would become austere, grave, and humorless men. They would carry within their hearts, as he did in his, the burden of the sins of Israel. These men joined John in his titanic task of preparing the way for the coming of God's own Messiah.

To hear John was to hear the unexpected, for each day was different. Each day John spoke, and each time he spoke he addressed something the crowd had never heard anyone else say. His daring, his fearlessness in broaching any topic, awed the multitude *and* his disciples.

On one particularly hot day, when the crowds seemed to stretch to the horizon, John cried out, "The day after the next

Sabbath I will go to the Jordan River. There I will immerse beneath the Jordan waters all who have repented of their way of life. I will immerse all who make their lives ready for the coming of the Lord."

It was on that day John received a new name, a name which was soon to be on the lips of all Israel, for on that day he became known as John the Immerser.

Chapter 6

PEOPLE CAME TO HEAR JOHN because they were seeking something to fill a deep vacancy in their lives.

Merchants came to hear him and repented of their business practices and were then baptized in the fabled waters of the Jordan. Soldiers came, repented of their brutality, and were baptized. The camel drivers came, the farmers, the rustic fishermen, housewives, women of renown, women of the streets, all kinds and all classes came. And all who came, it seemed, came holding some secret sin, repented thereof, and disappeared beneath the Jordan waters.

Every Jew knew the ancient meaning of a soul's being plunged beneath the water of that particular river. It meant the end of life, the cessation of everything. Everyone awaiting baptism stood on the eastern bank, which was a foreign land. There they stepped into the water and disappeared . . . there to die. But each came up out of the water and stepped onto the western bank, safe within the border of the Promised Land, there to begin a new life with God. This simple drama was unforgettable.

There was one particular day at the Jordan that stood out from all others. It began with the arrival of horse-drawn carriages. A delegation of dignitaries had arrived. What important personages had come out to this obscure place?

It was the nation's religious leaders.

When John saw these costumed men, every muscle in his body became motionless. There was not one outer movement on his countenance to betray his inward feelings. As these religious dignitaries cut through the crowd, John watched as ordinary people dropped their heads or genuflected in a gesture of honor. This did not at all set well with the greatest nonconformist of all time.

John read every man as he stepped out of the carriages. Some had obviously come to sneer, to gather evidence against John, and to condemn. Others came with a great deal of uncertainty, hoping to discover for themselves whether or not John was a true prophet. There were even a few among them, the youngest, who came truly believing that John was a man of God. These young men hoped the older, more respected leaders might agree with their unspoken opinion. After all, if the older leaders gave their blessing to John, some of the young men knew they would be free to become his disciples.

But John saw more than this. He looked in the heart of every man now making his way through the midst of the crowd, and discerned the ultimate weakness of each one. There was not *one* among them brave enough, on his own, to break with accepted religious traditions.

The crowd continued giving way before these vaunted leaders. The delegation was on its way to the front of the crowd, to take their rightful place of honor. This was more than the desert prophet could ever hope to stomach. The religious system of his day, coming *here?* And daring to impose their abominable practices *here?* How dare they come! How dare they bring their arrogance, contempt, disdain, and pride to *this* place!

John had not come to this earth to compromise, nor to win over such men to the ways of God. After all, these men saw themselves as authorities in God's ways. John would not attempt to do the impossible: He would not call the leaders of the religious system to come out of that system. Yet the presence of these men was perverting the freedom that the baptized ones had gained as they laid aside the systemization of this world.

John, therefore, declared war. Open, unbridled, unquartered war . . . on Israel's most revered personages. He wanted every human being present to know how he felt about the chains that traditionalists had forged upon the hearts and souls of God's people. And just how did he feel? He felt this whole religious culture must perish.

There was nothing John could do better than thunder, and on this occasion he roared like a lion. Thrusting out the forefinger of one hand, he shattered earth and heaven with his denunciation.

"Who . . . who, I ask . . . who told you to repent?
"You nest of snakes, what are you doing here?"

The crowd was stunned. No one had *ever* talked this way to *these* men. Many in the crowd instinctively rose to their feet; after a moment, wide grins began to appear on the faces of some. But every eye was now riveted on the religious leaders. What would be their reaction? And, was it possible . . . had John committed some kind of blasphemy? The people knew the rumors about John being possessed of a demon; this was not going to help. They loved him for his boldness, yet no one ever dreamed he would take on the religious leaders of their nation. *No one* did that!

Shock turned to disbelief as John continued.

"I ask you again, you nest of snakes, who told you to turn away from the wrath that is coming on you?"

The religious leaders stopped. No one could speak to them in this way. After a brief moment, one of the leaders pulled his cloak up about him, turned, and whispered something to those nearest him. They, in turn, signaled to the others to make a sudden retreat.

But John was not finished.

"Your tree! An axe has been laid to your tree. The wrath of God is upon you. The axe will cut down your tree and destroy its root. The day is not far when all that you are shall be destroyed under the wrath of God."

With that the delegation, as one, gathered up their outer robes and hurried back toward their carriages, each devising in his heart some form of vengeance to take against John.

Someone in the crowd began to cheer. Someone else clapped. With that, the whole multitude stood and took up the applause. Everywhere men and women felt shackles falling from their souls. At last, someone had dared to challenge the religious system!

Spontaneously, the multitude moved toward John. It seemed that every soul present who had not been baptized wanted very much to do so now. They had all, as one, glimpsed something deeper of John's message, something they had never understood before.

It was a glorious day. Yet no one seemed to have laid hold of the obvious. Conduct like this would get John killed.

And then there was that other very memorable day.

Chapter 7

THE DOOR FROM THE OTHER realm opened, like a window, just over the Jordan River. Out from the very center of the being of God the Father came forth His own sacred Spirit, the Holy Spirit, somewhat as a dove might, fluttering out through the open door and coming to rest on one of the spectators who was listening to John speak.

John's eyes scanned the crowed, his fierce gaze catching every face. What was that? A light of unnatural origin, appearing out of nowhere, like a dove flying out of a window and coming to rest on someone out there in the crowd.

John realized he was seeing what no other eye could see. This was the sign of the Messiah. John fell silent. His only thought was, "Where landed the lighted dove? *Who* is out there?"

Murmuring whispers swept across the crowd. Many followed John's searching gaze.

Spontaneously, John roared,

"Behold the Lamb of God!

"I am nothing. This man is everything. Look no more to me; look to *him*. As for me, I am not even worthy to stoop down and unlatch the sandals that are on the feet of this one."

The Father seemed to agree. Standing in the door between the two realms, He called out.

"This is my beloved Son in whom I am well pleased."

And as God was pleased, so John was pleased. Nor did it bother John as he watched the multitudes forsake him and begin to follow Jesus. After all, John knew he had come into the world for this very reason.

What John did not know was that the easiest days of his work were now behind him. The harder were yet to come.

Chapter 8

"TELL ME OF MY COUSIN," asked John.

"Presently he is in Galilee. He, like you, has twelve disciples; there are also others, perhaps fifty or sixty more, who are always with him. He travels from town to town preaching."

The voice was that of Nadab, a follower of John's who had been in Galilee and witnessed Jesus' ministry.

"On occasions he speaks to large multitudes of people, but most of the time he speaks in someone's home."

"What does he speak about?"

"He mostly tells stories. And many of them have a great deal of humor in them."

Nadab paused. "Teacher, did you know he drinks? I mean, he drinks *wine*! And the twelve, his twelve, they are not like us. They laugh a lot.

"He receives many invitations to banquets. It seems he always accepts. Some say he eats too much and drinks too much or, at least, that his *disciples* do."

John's interest was intent, but his demeanor betrayed no evidence of his inward thoughts. Not one person present had the slightest idea what he thought of Nadab's report. It was a trait of John's that dated back to his childhood.

Nadab continued. "The people he keeps company with are mostly tax collectors, whores, and . . . well, people like that."

One of John's other disciples broke in with an observation. "Teacher, we have fasted almost to the point of starvation. We have prayed until our knees were sore. We follow your example in these things. You fast, you spend your life in prayer, you live a life of great restraint and discipline in all things. Your cousin tells stories, talks of lilies and birds, seeds and sheep, goes to banquets where he eats and drinks. He seems, in general, to be enjoying himself enormously. Some have even called him a drunkard and a glutton. Can you understand why some of us are a little confused?"

After a long pause, it became clear that John would not respond. Finally John took a deep breath and stood. "The people are waiting, and I have something important to say to them."

John walked out into the midst of the gathered multitude

and mounted a large stone. It was late afternoon. A cool breeze from the Sea of Galilee was blowing across the field. The sun was setting, and as it did, it bugled enormous golden rays across the sky.

John looked out across the people and called his heart to remember again his life's task: to bring Israel to full repentance, to level mountains, fill in the valleys, and prepare the way for God's final and greatest work upon the earth.

"Our king," cried John, "has taken unto himself his brother's wife. Herod has brought down the wrath of God upon himself. Nor will his wife Herodias be spared."

It would be no later than the next morning when Herod the Tetrarch would hear of John's denunciation. And when Herod heard, he went into a rage. But his rage was nothing compared to that of his new wife, for she vowed the darkest possible vengeance upon John the Baptizer. And in that craving for revenge, she screamed to her husband that John be arrested and thrown into a dungeon. Immediately! Nor did that mark the end of her wicked scheme.

Chapter 9

Protheus looked up to see the cause of the noise at the top of the stairs. He could make out the shadow of a prisoner standing between two Roman guards. Slowly, laboriously, the shackled prisoner made his way down the long, narrow stairwell.

Protheus could not help but think to himself, "I always imagined you to be a giant of a man; yet here, in this place, you seem in every way to be so ordinary. You appear . . . almost *vulnerable*."

The prisoner now came into full view. Protheus searched John's face, but like so many others, he could find not a single clue in this man's demeanor as to what his thoughts were. Was he afraid? anxious? hostile? Protheus was accustomed to being able to read a prisoner's emotions at this particular moment. But today *this* prisoner provided him nothing.

Protheus turned to one of the soldiers behind him.

"Cell three."

The soldier opened the iron-gated door; just beyond the grating, the cell dropped off into a pit some twelve feet deep. One of the soldiers was about to tie a rope around one of the bars and let himself down into the pit. Protheus interrupted.

"One moment. I will chain the prisoner." With that, Protheus turned to the two Roman guards and motioned for them to unshackle the prisoner. He then walked over to the cell door and let himself down into the rat-infested pit.

The place was dark, wet, and everything else that a dungeon was supposed to be. Protheus called up to the guards. "Step back from the prisoner.

"John, let yourself down here by that rope." John slipped the rope between his hands and lowered himself into the infernal pit.

"These chains fastened to the wall—I must clamp them to your feet and hands. The chains are long enough to allow you some movement. They are ordered from Herod. I am sorry to do this. You will remain in this prison until he decides what to do with you."

For several moments Protheus labored at the task of bolting the iron manacles around John's wrists and ankles. When finished, he stepped back.

"Three of your disciples have asked to see you. They will

be allowed to come next week. I understand they are bringing you some food."

Protheus grabbed the rope and was about to pull himself up. He paused, turned, and looked at John full on. "I have heard you speak in the wilderness. I regret . . ."

"It is all right," replied John. "The guilt is not yours."

With that Protheus pulled himself up to the floor above, closed the cell door, and addressed all the soldiers on duty.

"Listen to me. Within whatever bounds that damnable cell affords, you make this man comfortable; supply him with food and water and whatever else he needs. Meet his needs to the limits of the restrictions Herod has placed upon him. One more thing. I have clearly posted John's name on the wall beside his cell door. I want every man in this room to remember who it is in that pit."

A voice called out from the first cell. "What did you say? Have they brought John the Baptist to this place?"

Protheus sighed. He and every other man in the room knew what was coming next.

Chapter 10

"HEROD DID IT, DIDN'T HE? That damnable monster.

"John, is that you? Do you remember me? I was with you when you were but a child. Oh, I was a man of greatness then. Look at me now!

"Herod took my home; he took my money. Without a trial, without even a hearing! Then he threw me in this hellhole. Now Herod is the one who is rich! Rich on *my* wealth, and I am but a wretch. I swear a curse upon you, Herod . . . you monster . . . wicked man.

"I served him twenty years. Faithfully. No man has ever lived who has been so unjustly treated as I. It is unfair what he did, I tell you. Now look what that heinous man has done; the ogre has gone out and brought a prophet of God to this cursed place.

"I tell you, every problem, every pain, every sorrow in Judea finds its origin in Herod. There is no justice on this earth, no mercy . . . no pity. It is all his fault. All of it.

"John, can you hear me? Mark my word, you will rot here like the rest of us. Out there in your desert, you said one thing that is true. There is no end to the wickedness of the human heart. And Herod is the worst of all. I would be a happy, prosperous man today if it were not for that cold-blooded Herod, and the others . . . the others . . . *those* wicked men who conspired against me with him to take everything I had."

"Parnach, control your tongue," shouted one of the guards.

There was a pause. The prisoner in the first cell grew quiet. Unfortunately, though, his shouts had awakened the prisoner in the cell next to him.

Chapter 11

A THIN, BONY MAN MOVED up to the door of his cell and looked wildly into the eyes of the captain of the guards.

"John? Here? Are you telling me John is here in the prison of Machaerus? Are you telling me, Protheus, that he has been thrown into cell *three*, of all places?"

"Yes, Hannel, Herod has arrested John and had him brought here."

"Has God no pity? Has God no feelings?" asked Hannel in a cold, thin voice.

"Does devotion mean nothing to Him? *I* once trusted in God, just as John does. Are you really here, John? Do you remember me? I lived a devout and holy life before God. You remember, don't you, John? Well, look at what it has brought me. And you, see what devotion to God has brought *you*? Is this to be the end for men who have loved God and obeyed Him?

What kind of a God is it that will allow such things as we now suffer? God, You have thrown one of Your very own servants into a slimy hole!"

Hannel thrust one arm through the bars of his cell, clenched his fist, raised his face, and spat curses at God. He then ended his ravings with one last pronouncement. "Never again will I serve a God who treats men this way. When I needed Him, where was He? John, where is *your* God when you need Him the most?"

Not a single sound rose from the third cell. Whatever John might be thinking, he was keeping his own counsel. Protheus, on the other hand, could not help but wonder: "The prisoner in the first cell blames everything on men. The prisoner in the second cell blames everything on God. I wonder whom the prisoner in the third cell will blame. Man? God?

"Or perhaps his cousin?"

Chapter 12

THE SCENE IS A VILLAGE in Galilee called Nain. It is early evening. The streets of the town are packed with people waiting to bring their sick to Jesus.

Some of the infirm are blind, some crippled; one is deaf; another, frothing at the mouth, is held in restraint by his family. An anxious mother holds her small, fevered baby in her arms. Another mother cradles a crippled child in her lap. All manner of people are there, wracked by every disease known to man. All have one thing in common. They are seeking Jesus, hoping to receive healing or liberation at his hands.

The focal point of this crowd is a house located on one of the smaller streets of the village. In every direction the streets leading to this house are jammed with people. Walk through the courtyard and you will see that it, too, is filled.

There is pathos and anxiety everywhere. Perhaps the thing that makes the waiting ones most anxious is to hear a cry of joy coming from within the house and then, a moment later, watch someone depart, praising God for healing.

At this moment, three roughly dressed, leather-skinned men appear at the courtyard gate. One of the disciples of Jesus recognizes these men. He rushes into the house. Just as he is about to tell his master the news of the arrival of these men, a cripple rises on his feet, raises his hands to heaven, and cries out to God in praise for being cured.

"Lord, the disciples of John are here."

Jesus looked up. For one brief moment there was anxiety in his eyes.

"Please. Dismiss the people outside. Bring John's disciples here. Immediately."

With that, the Lord seated himself on the floor and waited pensively for the appearance of John's disciples.

In a moment, the three men solemnly took their place in front of Jesus. There was a long pause. Then Nadab broke the silence.

"We have come from John. He is in prison. Herod had him arrested for . . ."

"Yes, I know," replied the Lord.

"A few days ago we were allowed to visit our teacher. He is

chained inside a filthy pit. There are rumors that it will not be long before Herod has him killed."

There was a pause. Nadab waited to see if Jesus had some response to this word.

"John sent us to you, to ask you a question. It was the only request he made of us. We have traveled far to find you, yet it is but for the answer to one question that we come."

Again Nadab paused. Again no one spoke.

"Teacher, the question that John would ask of you is this." Nadab paused again, his face flushed. "John's question is, 'Are you the Messiah, or should we look for another?'"

A long, stunned silence followed. Pain was felt in the heart of every man in the room. You could read it in the faces of John's three disciples, it was evident upon the faces of the twelve, but it was most evident upon the face of the Lord himself.

Jesus sighed deeply. For one brief moment, he dropped his head in what seemed to be a gesture of anguish. Looking up again, he addressed the question.

"Nadab, return to John. Tell him, for me, these things.

"First, tell John that the blind see, the lame walk, and the deaf hear.

"Then tell my cousin that the gospel is proclaimed—not

only proclaimed but received with gladness—and that men and women are being set free."

The Lord paused, took a deep, labored breath. Then slowly, purposefully, he continued. "Lastly, Nadab, tell John . . . tell John . . ."

The Lord's voice choked for a moment. Pain was in his words. "Tell my brother John:

"And blessed is he who is not offended with me."

There was another pause. Jesus stood, embraced the three men, and then turned to his disciples. "The hour is very late. It is time we departed here. We must go on to the next village. Please dismiss those waiting outside."

John's three disciples stood, stunned. After a long moment of obvious confusion, they turned and made their departure. The courtyard they crossed was now empty, as were the streets they passed through.

Tomorrow will hold for Jesus yet another village. For the disciples of John, tomorrow will hold the enigma of this day.

But what will tomorrow hold for those who were sent home that evening? They all departed without being healed. And John? What will be his response to the strange words of his cousin?

Chapter 13

THE THREE DISCIPLES OF JOHN squatted down on the slimy floor of the dungeon that had become John's home.

"Teacher, we have seen your cousin."

"Did you ask my question?"

"We did."

"And his answer?"

"Teacher, the answer is very strange. We do not understand it."

John sighed. It was as though he knew this would be Nadab's response.

"His reply?"

"Teacher, he said to tell you that the blind and the dumb and the crippled receive sight and hearing and healing. Then he said to tell you that the good news is proclaimed, and received with joy."

John turned those words over in his mind very slowly. After

several minutes, his brow wrinkled. The prisoner leaned forward and asked, "Is that all?"

"No, teacher, he said one other thing, and then he dismissed the crowd and bade us farewell. What he said was, 'Tell John, "And blessed is he who is not offended with me."'"

There was a long silence as three men studied the face of John, hoping to glimpse his reaction to these words. But, as always, there was none.

Finally John queried: "Where was my cousin?"

"In a village in Galilee, called Nain," responded Nadab. "There were sick people everywhere; streets, lanes, and alleys were all filled with people wanting to be healed. The place was overrun with suffering souls."

"Were they being healed?"

"Yes, teacher, many were being healed."

With those words, John's interest quickened, his frame straightened. "Did you say, *many*?" responded John.

"Yes, teacher, many."

"Many?" asked John again.

Nadab was puzzled. "Yes, teacher," he answered again, "*Many* were being healed."

"Many," repeated John quietly as to himself. Then he leaned forward again. "Many, Nadab? Many, but *not* all?"

For a brief instant Nadab was at a loss as to what John was saying. Then his own eyes lit up, revealing the shock of what John was observing. "Yes, teacher, you are right. There were many who were being healed, but not *all*."

". . . *not* . . . all."

John stared vacantly into space. Had he at last found the answer to the questions which had troubled him so deeply about Jesus? Or had he simply added more questions to his dilemma?

At that very moment, there was someone else who was struggling with this same dilemma.

Chapter 14

"LEAVE ME," SAID JESUS to his companions.

With those words, Jesus wandered off to a sequestered place to be alone. Never before in all his thirty-one years, nor in all his preexistence in eternity, had he ever longed so intensely to answer the cry and the question of someone struggling to understand the mysterious ways of his God.

If ever there was a time for him to give a clear answer, if ever there was a person to whom he should speak clearly, surely the time was now and the person, John. If any man ever lived who had a right to have an explanation given to him, that man was his own flesh and blood, his only cousin.

"John, your pain is great. I feel it. Tonight you so desperately need to understand me, to fathom my ways, to peer into the riddle of my sovereignty. Your heart is breaking. But, John, you are not the first to have this need. You are but one in a long train of humankind stretching across all the centuries of man who have called out to me with questions and doubts. You are but one voice among so many who wonder and who agonize over my ways."

With those words spoken, a scene of an event that had taken place long ago began to emerge before the eyes of the Lord.

Jesus shuddered. Before him was Egypt. The Lord of time stepped into the streets of the city of Pharaoh. "I have been here before. I have walked down these streets, listening to the quiet cries, the murmurings, the prayers of my own people . . . held here in slavery."

The Lord paused and looked about. He could clearly hear every prayer being prayed. They seemed to be lifted up to him in harmony with their rustling chains.

"You who are descendants of a man named Jacob, you have cried out to me so long, suffered so long, and wept so long. You have lifted your faces to heaven for years without number. But the heavens are stone. It appears your God has gone deaf. You have been born in slavery. You have grown up, cried out for freedom, and then died, without your prayers being answered. Your children came along to take your place, were fettered with the same worn chains of their fathers. They, too, cried out for deliverance, and they, too, died with their chains still forged to their wrists."

The Lord walked on.

"Your children's children have grown old. They have come to me with their prayers myriads of times, calling out, 'God deliver us from the Pharaoh, deliver us from this slave master who does not know our father, Joseph. Oh, our God, lead us back to our homeland.'

"But I did not answer, not so much as one word. And so it continued for you and your offspring . . . for twelve generations.

"I left you in slavery for almost four hundred years. Never once in all that time were your prayers answered. You cried out to me, but I did not respond. No clear word, no insight into my ways, no explanation of my purposes, no reasons were given why I did not answer your cries. Your hearts were broken before me.

"But my heart was broken with yours.

"After four hundred years, there were still men and women who were believing in me! After four hundred years of not hearing from me, still you believed!"

At that moment came a piercing cry. It was the voice of a mother.

"Oh, God, if You are there, will You not answer? Tomorrow

this beautiful child will be taken from my arms, forever. He will be shackled, enslaved, and forever doomed to make bricks beside the river Nile. I will die never to see my child again. He will grow old and die in the chains they forge upon his wrists tomorrow. Will You not hear my cry?"

The eyes of the Lord filled with tears.

"Oh, Israel, you are confronted with one simple fact.

"Oh woman, you, like all those before you . . . you, like my cousin John, rotting in a pit . . . have come face to face with one stark truth.

"Your God has not lived up to your expectations."

Chapter 15

THE SCENE CHANGED. Once more the place was Egypt, but it was many years into the future. On this occasion, the Lord of time stepped into an unfolding drama that was a scene, not of slavery, but of death.

Women were frantically running down the streets, with Egyptian solders in pursuit. Every newborn Hebrew male child would be slain that day. That is, all but one. The one lone survivor would grow up to save Israel from Egypt. But these panic-stricken mothers did not know this. They would live out their entire lives without even one of them ever knowing that eighty years hence God would avenge the death of their children and set Israel free.

"They do not know," he sighed. "They *will* know, but not here on this earth. All they will ever know in this lifetime is that I did not come to them in their hour of greatest need. Today they, like all others, have met a God they do not understand.

"So it has been in all the past, so it will be throughout all ages to come."

The scene changed again. The Lord of space and time was back in Galilee again, alone. Once more he spoke.

"If I ever cared for those who lived in slavery in Egypt; if I ever cared for Job on his ash heap, or Jeremiah in his miry pit; if I ever cared for my people when the armies of Nebuchadnezzar surrounded Jerusalem and carried them off to slavery; if I ever longed to give answer and explanation; if there were one day above all others that I would speak, today would be that day.

"This day I have flesh and blood. I have a human mother who loved Elizabeth and who loves Elizabeth's son. She does not wish to see him die, and like all others, she wants so much to understand. Today I have brothers; I have sisters. I am an earthen man, with blood coursing through my veins, with human emotions, with family responsibilities. John and I are the elder sons of our two families. It is with human eyes I watch this unholy deed of Herod. Nor is that all. Everywhere I look I see my people caught up in circumstances not of their own making.

"If ever there has been a moment I have longed to answer the questions of any man or woman, it is now. And it is to you, John, I want to give an explanation of my ways.

"John, I watched you walk into that desert as a twelve-year-old child. I saw your days turn to weeks and your weeks turn into years, as you fasted, as you ate the scraps of the desert, as you clothed yourself with the desert's waste. I have watched your soft skin turn to leather. I have seen you age inordinately. Your faithfulness to me is without parallel. Not since Eve bore her first man-child has there ever been one like unto you.

"I gave you a task greater than the one I gave to Moses. You are a prophet greater than any who has ever come before.

"But, most of all, you are my kin. You are my own flesh and blood.

"If ever, ever I have wanted to give answer to a man's questions, to explain my sovereign ways, it is today. Yet I have been to you, as to all others, a Lord *not* fully understood, a God who rarely makes clear exactly what He is doing in the life of one of His children.

"Angels shall plea
to set thee free,
Death shall weep
when he comes for thee,
Yet ne'er shall an answer come
from me."

Chapter 16

As DAY DAWNED IN the village of Nain, the multitude that had gathered there the night before received an unbearable shock. Jesus had departed the village the night before, soon after he dismissed the crowd for the evening. He was gone, and *no* one knew where.

That morning a mother, who had come all the way from Damascus carrying her crippled child, would begin the long trek back home, still carrying a beloved child with a never-to-be-healed twisted foot. Throughout all the rest of her long life this mother would wonder why the Lord had not waited just a few more moments before dismissing the crowd, for she was next in line.

"And blessed are you
if you are not offended with me."

That same morning, an old man was guided back to his home by a friend, there to ever wonder, until the day he died, what sight might have been like if only he had been able to reach the master healer just a few minutes earlier. But his destiny would forever be a life of darkness . . . and wondering.

"And blessed is he
who is not offended with me."

A mother will return home with her young daughter who will forever remain disfigured because of a childhood accident. Throughout that despondent day and on into the following weeks and years, that mother will look down into the face of her child and often hear her ask why she was not healed that day in Galilee. "After all, Mother, so many others were."

The mother will give first one answer and then another; those answers will satisfy neither mother nor daughter. Both will forever wonder why the Lord left them that evening, not caring enough for them to remain just a little longer. The mother will die and go to her grave; her daughter will grow up to womanhood carrying her disfigurement throughout her life.

"And blessed is that one
who is not offended with me."

A sick baby will die. An epileptic child will go on having seizures as long as he lives. A fevered young girl will suffer weeks of pain before she regains her health. A deaf mute will spend the rest of his life begging at the city gate. These and many others, with even more tragic stories, departed the village of Nain that morning . . . each so downcast that words could not express their feelings of hopelessness. Worst of all, from God came no explanation concerning His ways.

Many were healed. But not all.

"And blessed is he
who is not offended with me."

Chapter 17

PROTHEUS PUSHED OPEN the heavy prison door and stepped out into the sunlight to escape the stench of the dungeon and, for a moment, to breathe fresh air. Immediately the music from Herod's palace caught his ear. Herod was giving a huge banquet for his friends that evening. "Honoring his own birthday!" recalled Protheus. There would be revelry. There would be . . .

Suddenly a cold chill gripped Protheus.

It would be just like Herod . . . to haul John the Baptist up to the banquet hall to make sport of him!

"That is exactly what he will do."

Protheus whirled around and rushed back into the prison. . . . He wanted to warn John about what might happen to him before the evening was over. But before he could reach John's cell, Protheus felt a strong hand on his shoulder. He turned. It was one of Herod's personal bodyguards.

"It's John, is it not? You have come for John. Herod is going to make sport of him."

"Far worse than that," replied the bodyguard, betraying his own apprehension. "Far, far worse than that. Salome, the daughter of Herod's wife, has just danced for the guests. Herod is drunk, and in his stupor he offered Salome anything she wanted, up to half his kingdom. She, in turn, inquired of her mother just what to ask for in the presence of so lucrative an offer." The bodyguard paused.

"Protheus, it seems that tonight Herod's guests will *not* be entertained by making sport of John the Baptist. No, it will be far more macabre than that. John's head is to be brought into the banquet room on a platter!"

Protheus lost his balance; his eyesight blurred. The bodyguard grabbed his arm and steadied him. "The same thing happened to me when I heard," observed the guard.

"What now?" asked Protheus.

"I would say John has less than five minutes to live. Bring him to me."

"May the gods have mercy on us," whispered Protheus. "And if there be but one God, and if that God be the God of the Jews, we would be fools to believe He would show pity on us for what we are about to do."

Chapter 18

"John, they have come for you. Much sooner than you had thought. In a few minutes you will be no more. There is no time to send word to your disciples. Nor to my mother, Mary, who has worried so much for your safety. You will not be given opportunity of even a single word to anyone. Nor will you be able to ask again the question you addressed to me.

"In less than four minutes now, you will be dead. How many thoughts can be crowded into one's mind in four minutes? How many doubts? How many questions? Not many. But, John, worst of all, there will be *no* answers.

"And blessed are you, John,
if you are not offended with me.

"They have unshackled you. The staircase is before you. The door above is open. You can see the light of day above you.

"Why is this happening to you, John? You, of all people? Your head . . . *severed* from your body? Why? Because of an obscene dance by a teenage girl. How ironic.

"You will never live to see your thirty-third birthday, nor will you know exactly why I have called you. Nor will you know if your life on this earth counted for anything. Those long years in the searing desert, you denied yourself of everything this earth affords except food and water, and only enough of that to keep you alive. You did this all for me. Yet, as you face death, there is no evidence that your life was anything but wasted. Have I forsaken you in the hour you need me most?

"And blessed are you
if you are not offended with me.

"You have reached the head of the stairs. You are not sure which way they would have you turn. A guard points to the left. You follow. Is this happening? You have less than one minute before that immutable blank. You recall those long vigils before my face. Did you misunderstand me? Were you mistaken? Perhaps you did not hear my voice at all?

"In all those years you lived alone in the desert you never once knew love or comfort from another human being. Will I not extend such comfort to you now, at last? You never had the pleasure of your own children to climb up on your lap, to give you earthly joy. You never came in contact with a woman, ever; you never had a wife. You have never known intimate love. You have never even had a friend. Your whole life was lived for your calling, and for me. Will I not now, in this last moment of your life, part the veil and allow you to see something . . . anything . . . of my purpose in your life and in your death? You will die wondering why I ate and drank as I did, why I did not fast as you fasted, nor pray as you prayed. Was the Messiah not to be a man of sorrows and acquainted with grief?

"You will die today at the hands of unclean, uncircumcised, heathen, Gentile Romans. But your death at their hands will come about only by my sovereign permission. And you will die not understanding why I allowed this seemingly senseless act.

"And blessed are you
if you are not offended with me.

"You will not see the multitudes cry out in jubilation at my entry into Jerusalem. Neither will you see me crucified, nor hear of my resurrection and my triumph over death. You will die not knowing that you have proclaimed the coming of no less than the *Son of God.*

"Death is but a few seconds away, and still there is no answer to your question. You will die not understanding.

"And blessed are you, John,
if you are not offended with me.

"They have opened the gate to the courtyard. There it is, the block on which you will lay your head, and there the man who will take your life. You will be remembered as one of the greatest men who ever lived. But you will not know that, nor will you hear the Son of God say, 'Of men born of women, there was none greater than John.'

"Even now as you kneel, you wonder if you are a complete failure. You gave so much, poured out your life so completely, lived for God so singularly. Yet, despite all this, you could not so much as win the favor of God to the point of His giving you one answer to one question. It was, after all, the only request you ever made.

"I did not give to you an answer. I never have. The question of *why* always remains unanswered in all my dealings with men; this is my way. But if there were one human being on this earth to whom I would make clear my purpose, it would be *you*. And it would be now. Above all other men or women who have ever lived, I would give an answer to *you*."

John knelt and placed his head upon the block.

"When I called you, John, and told you that you would announce the coming of the Messiah, you assumed that because you were going to prepare the way for me, you would have the joy of seeing that wonderful day of my coming in glory. But today you have met a God you do not understand. Such is the mystery of my sovereignty. Such are my ways in *every* generation. No man has ever understood me, not fully. No man ever will. I will always be something other than what men expect me to be. I will work out my will in ways different from what men foresee.

"The guard has shifted his weight. The blade is raised above you. Death stands beside you. Die, my brother John, in the presence of a God who did not live up to your expectations.

"And blessed are you
if you are not offended with me."

Shall we scorn that God has revealed so little concerning His ways, or rejoice that He has revealed so much?

Chapter 19

A DAY LIKE THAT WHICH awaited John awaits us all. It is unavoidable because every believer imagines his God to be a certain way, and is quite sure his Lord will do certain things under certain conditions. But your Lord is never quite what you imagined Him to be.

You have now come face to face with a God whom you do not fully understand. You have met a God who has not lived up to your expectations. Every believer must come to grips with a God who did not do things quite the way it was expected.

You are going to get to know your Lord by faith or you will not know Him at all. Faith in Him, trust that is in *Him . . . not* in His ways.

Today you are resentful of those who so callously hurt you. But no, not really. The truth is you are angry with God because, ultimately, you are not dealing with men, you are dealing with the sovereign hand of your Lord. Behind all events, behind all things, there is always His sovereign hand.

The question is not, "Why is God doing this? Why is He like this?" The question is not, "Why does He not answer me?" The question is not, "I need Him desperately; why does He not come rescue me?" The question is not, "Why did God allow this tragedy to happen to me, to my children, to my wife, to my husband, to my family?" Nor is it, "Why does God allow injustices?"

The question before the house is this: "Will you follow a God you do not understand? Will you follow a God who does not live up to your expectations?"

Your Lord has put something in your life which you cannot bear. The burden is simply too great. He was never supposed to do *this*! But the question remains, "Will you continue to follow this God who did not live up to your expectations?"

"And blessed are you
if you are not offended with me."

Epilogue

"CAPTAIN, THE THIRD CELL IS EMPTY."

"It will not be empty long. I have just received word that we are to receive a new prisoner."

"What has this one done?"

"I do not know. There is always the possibility this one is as innocent as was John."

The soldier's response was simple. "I hate having such prisoners! We have a prisoner in the first cell who rails against unfairness, against men, and against circumstances. We have a prisoner in the second cell who is hostile toward God because of what his God has done to him. . . ."

"The new prisoner has arrived," called a voice at the head of the stairs.

"Take the rope," said Protheus to the guard. "Lower the prisoner into the miry pit."

Who is this prisoner? Who is this one who will now be

imprisoned in the third cell? What name will be inscribed beside the cell door?

One thing is certain: It was inevitable that this person be sent here. Inevitable, unavoidable, and a sovereign act of God.

The prisoner's name? Surely, the question is not necessary, dear reader; *you* are the prisoner in the third cell!

> "And blessed are you
> if you are not offended with me."

"Cousin?"

"Yes, John."

"Jesus?"

"Yes, John. It is I."

"My Lord and my God . . . but I had so many questions as I faced death!"

"So did I when I faced death. Just as I did not answer you, neither did my Father answer me. We died in quite similar ways."

"You died? You died as ignominiously, as I did?"

"Yes, John. But I rose from the dead."

"You rose from the dead? But how?

"Come, brother John . . . take my hand. The moment has come. I will now take you to that place where you know . . . even as you are known."

Dear reader, no one can fully understand the pain you feel as you suffer your present situation. Whether it came upon you because of circumstances or by the deeds of men, one thing is certain. Before this present tragedy entered into your life, it first passed through the sovereign hand of God.

"And blessed are you . . ."

Book Discussion Guide

1. Look at pages 17–19, which describe John's absolute devotion to God, unimpeded by cares of this world. What would you require, or what thorns would you need to pull from your life (see Luke 8.14), to live unhindered before God?

2. We remember John for many things, not least Jesus' praise in Matthew 11:11: "Of all who have ever lived, none is greater than John the Baptist." But in this story, John never felt his ministry was great. What's your opinion of your own legacy? How do you expect people will remember you?

3. How do you generally react to nonconformists—people who don't fit in by nature or by choice? How does your immediate community respond to them? How welcome are they in your church?

4. How can we recognize a person of God? What are the hallmarks to look for, and how can we avoid looking at the wrong factors?

5. John railed against the Pharisees, who had burdened the people with man-made religious rules. Are there any religious or social systems today that might prevent people from connecting with God? What can you do to change or oppose those systems?

6. John answered God's calling and, though he had questions, never looked back. What is God calling you to do? How can you be wholehearted?

7. Has God ever failed to meet your expectations? How did you respond to Him? What happened in your relationship with Him as a result?

8. Why did Hannel and Parnach land in the first and second cells? How did they respond to their predicaments? What is your response when you face adversity or trouble?

9. When John's disciples brought his question to Jesus (pp. 48–50), what caused Jesus such anguish? Do you think Jesus has ever had a similar response to your own doubts or anxious fears?

10. Reread chapter 16. How do you respond to a God we do not understand, who is capable of healing many but does not heal all? Have you ever been offended with

God? If so, what are the standards to which you were holding God? Why do you think He remains so difficult to understand?

11. Think of a time when you've prayed or pleaded and the only answer has been silence. How did this affect your relationship with God? What do you think God was saying by remaining silent?

12. "I will always be something other than what men expect me to be. I will work out my will in ways different from what men foresee" (p. 73). Do you agree with the author's proposition? What can we know of God? What sort of assumptions about Him should we avoid?

13. Do you trust your understanding of God, or do you trust God Himself (ch. 19)? When is it easy to confuse the two?

Please turn the page for an excerpt from
A Tale of Three Kings . . .

Chapter 1

THE YOUNGEST SON of any family bears two distinctions: He is considered to be both spoiled and uninformed. Usually little is expected of him. Inevitably, he displays fewer characteristics of leadership than the other children in the family. As a child, he never leads. He only follows, for he has no one younger on whom to practice leadership.

So it is today. And so it was three thousand years ago in a village called Bethlehem, in a family of eight boys. The first seven sons of Jesse worked near their father's farm. The youngest was sent on treks into the mountains to graze the family's small flock of sheep.

On those pastoral jaunts, this youngest son always carried two things: a sling and a small, guitarlike instrument. Spare time for a sheepherder is abundant on rich mountain plateaus where sheep can graze for days in one sequestered meadow. But as time passed and days became weeks, the young man became very lonely. The feeling of friendlessness that always roamed inside him was magnified. He often cried. He also played his harp a great deal. He had a good voice, so he often sang. When these activities failed to comfort him, he gathered up a pile of stones and, one by one, swung them at a distant tree with something akin to fury.

When one rock pile was depleted, he would walk to the blistered tree, reassemble his rocks, and designate another leafy enemy at yet a farther distance.

He engaged in many such solitary battles.

This shepherd-singer-slinger also loved his Lord. At night, when all the sheep lay sleeping and he sat staring at the dying fire, he would strum upon his harp and break into quiet song. He sang the ancient hymns of his forefathers' faith. While he sang he wept, and while weeping he often broke out in abandoned praise—until mountains in distant places lifted up his praise and tears and passed them on to higher mountains, until they eventually reached the ears of God.

When the young shepherd did not praise and when he did not cry, he tended to each and every sheep and lamb. When not occupied with his flock, he swung his companionable sling and swung it again and again until he could tell every rock precisely where to go.

Once, while singing his lungs out to God, angels, sheep, and passing clouds, he spied a living enemy: a huge bear! He lunged forward. Both found themselves moving furiously toward the same small object, a lamb feeding at a table of rich, green grass. Youth and bear stopped halfway and whirled to face one another. Even as he instinctively reached into his pocket for a stone, the young man realized, "Why, I am not afraid."

Meanwhile, brown lightning on mighty, furry legs charged at the shepherd with foaming madness. Impelled by the strength of youth, the young man married rock to leather, and soon a brook-smooth pebble whined through the air to meet that charge.

A few moments later, the man—not quite so young as a moment before—picked up the little lamb and said, "I am your shepherd, and God is mine."

And so, long into the night, he wove the day's saga into a song. He hurled that hymn to the skies again and again until he had taught the melody and words to every angel that had ears. They, in turn, became custodians of this wondrous song and passed it on as healing balm to brokenhearted men and women in every age to come.

Chapter 2

A FIGURE IN THE DISTANCE was running toward him. It grew and became his brother. "Run!" cried the brother. "Run with all your strength. I'll watch the flock."

"Why?"

"An old man, a sage. He wants to meet all eight of the sons of Jesse, and he has seen all but you."

"But why?"

"Run!"

So David ran. He stopped long enough to get his breath. Then, sweat pouring down his sunburned cheeks, his red face matching his red curly hair, he walked into his father's house, his eyes recording everything in sight.

The youngest son of Jesse stood there, tall and strong, but more in the eyes of the curious old gentleman than to anyone else in the room. Kith and kin cannot always tell when a man is grown, even when looking straight at him. The elderly man saw. And something more he saw. In a way he himself did not understand, the old man knew what God knew.

God had taken a house-to-house survey of the whole kingdom in search of someone very special. As a result of this survey, the Lord God Almighty had found that this leather-lunged troubadour loved his Lord with a purer heart than anyone else on all the sacred soil of Israel.

"Kneel," said the bearded one with the long, gray hair. Almost regally, for one who had never been in that particular position, David knelt and then felt oil pouring down on his head. Somewhere, in one of the closets of his mind labeled "childhood information," he found a thought: *This is what men do to designate royalty! Samuel is making me a . . . what?*

The Hebrew words were unmistakable. Even children knew them.

"Behold the Lord's anointed!"

Quite a day for that young man, wouldn't you say? Then do you find it strange that this remarkable event led the young man not to the throne but to a decade of hellish agony and suffering? On that day, David was enrolled, not into the lineage of royalty but into the school of brokenness.

Samuel went home. The sons of Jesse, save one, went forth

to war. And the youngest, not yet ripe for war, received a promotion in his father's home . . . from sheepherder to messenger boy. His new job was to run food and messages to his brothers on the front lines. He did this regularly.

On one such visit to the battlefront, he killed another bear, in exactly the same way as he had the first. This bear, however, was nine feet tall and bore the name Goliath. As a result of this unusual feat, young David found himself a folk hero.

And eventually he found himself in the palace of a mad king. And in circumstances that were as insane as the king, the young man was to learn many indispensable lessons.

Chapter 3

DAVID SANG TO THE MAD KING. Often. The music helped the old man a great deal, it seems. And all over the palace, when David sang, everyone stopped in the corridors, turned their ears in the direction of the king's chamber, and listened and wondered. How did such a young man come to possess such wonderful words and music?

Everyone's favorite seemed to be the song the little lamb had taught him. They loved that song as much as did the angels.

Nonetheless, the king was mad, and therefore he was jealous. Or was it the other way around? Either way, Saul felt threatened by David, as kings often do when there is a popular, promising young man beneath them. The king also knew, as did David, that this boy just might have his job some day.

But would David ascend to the throne by fair means or foul?

Saul did not know. This question is one of the things that drove the king mad.

David was caught in a very uncomfortable position; however, he seemed to grasp a deep understanding of the unfolding drama in which he had been caught. He seemed to understand something that few of even the wisest men of his day understood. Something that in our day, when men are wiser still, even fewer understand.

And what was that?

God did not have—but wanted very much to have—men and women who would live in pain.

God wanted a broken vessel.

GENE EDWARDS was born and raised in east Texas, the son of an oil-field roughneck. He was converted to Christ in his junior year in college. He graduated from East Texas State University in Commerce, Texas, at the age of eighteen, with majors in English literature and history. His first year of postgraduate work was taken at the Baptist Theological Seminary in Ruschlikon, Switzerland. He received his master's degree in theology from Southwestern Baptist Theological Seminary in Ft. Worth, Texas at the age of twenty-two. He served as a Southern Baptist pastor and then as an evangelist for ten years.

Today his ministry includes conferences on the deeper Christian life and on living that life in the context of a practical experience of church life. There have been seventy translations of his books in eighteen languages.

Gene and his wife, Helen, now make their home in Jacksonville, Florida. The author can be reached at the following address:

Gene Edwards
P. O. Box 3450
Jacksonville, FL 32206
www.geneedwards.com

A Tale of Three Kings and its sequel, *The Prisoner in the Third Cell*, have become modern Christian classics, and readers everywhere have acclaimed *The Divine Romance* as one of the finest pieces of Christian literature of our time and a magnificent saga that will take your breath away. Here is an incomparable love story told in almost childlike simplicity, yet revealing some of the deepest truths of the Christian faith.

Also in the same genre is the spellbinding story of the history of God's people . . . as seen by the angels—The Chronicles of Heaven series (*The Beginning, The Escape, The Birth, The Triumph, The Return*). In addition, The First-Century Diaries series presents the sweeping panorama of the entire saga of the first-century church.

Gene Edwards has written three books that serve as an introduction to the deeper Christian life: *Living by the Highest Life, The Secret to the Christian Life*, and *The Inward Journey*. For a complete list of books by Gene Edwards, see the page opposite the title page.

Three modern classics by Gene Edwards

A tyrant, a usurper, a willing vessel.

"You cannot tell who is the Lord's anointed and who is not."

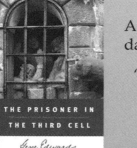

A man of God imprisoned in the darkest of places: his own doubts.

"Will you follow a God who does not live up to your expectations?"

The greatest love story ever told.

"Turn back, O City. Turn back, O bride of God."